Never Give a

Duck a Pen

CHRIS WHITE

2000

2010

A Decade of Daftness

First published in Great Britain in 2010
by Caboodle Books Ltd
Copyright © Chris White 2010

A Catalogue record for this book is available
from the British Library.

ISBN 978 0 9565 239 4 5

Cover and Illustrations by Chris White
Page Layout by Highlight Type Bureau Ltd
Printed by Cox and Wyman

The paper and board used in the paperback by
Caboodle Books Ltd are natural recyclable products
made from wood grown in sustainable forests.
The manufacturing processes conform to the environmental
regulations of the country of origin.

Caboodle Books Ltd
Riversdale, 8 Rivock Avenue, Steeton, BD20 6SA
www.authorsabroad.com

Order of Service

CHRIS WHITE

2000

2010

A Decade of Daftness

Bitey the Veggie Vampire

Bitey was a vampire,
Who wasn't very good.
He couldn't stand the taste of meat,
Or the smell of blood.

Whilst his vampire friends ran wild in the dark,
Bitey could not find his niche.
As they bit necks and ate human flesh,
Bitey just fancied some quiche.

The outfit was right, the gothic clothes,
It was Halloween when he was born.
If only the necks he was meant to devour,
Were made from some Tofu or Quorn.

Bitey tried to be evil,
To cause a bit more of a fright,
So off he set, fangs glistening,
Into the summer's night...

When the sun rose though, the truth became clear,
Bitey had not left his mark.
The most daring act he'd committed all night?
He ate a parsnip in the dark!

The other vampires just laughed at him,
None of them understood,
That even if Bitey grazed his own knee
He'd faint at the sight of his blood.

"But my diet's healthy!" he protested.
"I feel fine, and I suppose,
I save money on dry cleaning
With no blood stains on my clothes."

Alas Bitey's story does not finish well,
It does not finish well at all.
The malfunctioning vampire's aversion to meat,
Was in the end, to be his downfall.

You see, Bitey was slain, just last week,
And his whole world fell apart.
He was found late at night, when the moon was bright,
With a 12 ounce steak through his heart...

Never Give a Duck a Pen

Never give a duck a pen,
Decline him without being rude.
For although it looks like he wants to write,
He really just thinks that it's food.

Never give a fish a pen,
Not even if it demands.
It just goes to remind them,
That they've not got any hands.

Never give a leopard a pen,
No matter what it says.
All it'll do is just lie around,
And play join up the dots for days.

Never give a bat a pen,
Even though it sounds exciting.
Because it lives in a dark, black cave,
It can't see what it's writing.

But give a pen to a monkey,
And with a bit of luck,
Give him a few days and he'll
Probably write this book!

Hello!

Hi! Hello! How are you?
I hope you are ok.
Thanks a lot for finding time
To read my poems today.

There's tales of slugs and centipedes,
An ugly baby, a dead cat,
A shark, an armadillo, a vampire
And, wait...did you hear that?

Something scuttled across the floor...
Look! It's over there!
With two big eyes, eight long legs,
And short, black, spiky hair.

I think it is a Pidey.
The horriblest of creatures,
That creeps round in the shadows,
Just ask your mums and teachers.

I think it's winking at me
And sticking out its tongue!
Pideys make me nervous,
But we have to carry on...

We'll try to continue as best we can,
But PLEASE keep your eye out,
And if you see one anywhere,
Be sure to stand and shout:

"PIDEY! PIDEY! PIDEY!"

Zola

Zola is a show squirrel
Who loves to sing and dance.
She can merengue and do the cha-cha
On each and every branch!

The woodland creatures love to watch her
As she performs with style and guts.
The rabbits are all ears, the owls have a hoot
And the squirrels just go nuts!!

Gordon

Gordon was a tiny flea
Who had trouble every year.
You see, his family was so big,
Buying presents was very dear.

He had four hundred siblings,
That's a birthday every day!
So when time came to get them gifts
Gordon couldn't afford to pay.

But this year it's not so expensive,
'Cause of the shop he found.
Now his brothers and sisters each get a gift
From *'Everything's a Pound'*.

Stumpy

He's only got one little leg,
His feathers are matted and lumpy,
He's the mankiest pigeon you ever did see
And he goes by the name of Stumpy.

His beak is blunt, his eyes are dull,
His wings are weak and frail,
His breath smells of unpleasant things
And there's pigeon poo on his tail.

Stumpy lives in the market place
With his pigeon friends,
They spend all day hunting for chips
Amongst the old fag ends.

"How come one leg?" I hear you ask.
It's because he was hit by a cab
Whilst trying to cross the inner ring road
To eat a discarded kebab.

He'll sit with his pals on the top of statues
But if one of them should cough,
Stumpy, because of his lack of both legs,
Will more than likely fall off.

Because Stumpy can't run very fast
And it's such an effort to fly,
He'll be left bruised and battered because someone has,
Kicked him as they walked by.

Even though most pigeons are just one big pain,
That always get in the way
Stumpy's not like that; he's not like the rest,
He's the one pigeon that is OK!

So the next time you're out in the City
And you see a bird who's a bit jumpy,
Don't run and shout "Shoo!" ...do his legs number two?
As it might be the bird they call Stumpy!

Duck in a Hat

A duck waddled into my room today,
Sat down on the bed and looked like it would stay.
It was wearing a tie and a small bowler hat,
It stared right towards me and...wait...what was that?

Er...anyway...this duck switched the radio on,
And started to sing its favourite song.
I thought it was strange as it moved up beside me
And...HANG ON! LOOK! THERE!!!

PIDEY! PIDEY! PIDEY!

Something Smells

"Something smells. What can it be?"
Little Bobby said.
"Is it me or is it you?"
"Nope. The gerbil's dead."

Bleaty KaBoom the Sheep of Doom!

What's that sound? Can you hear it?
BAAA! KABOOM! BAAA! KABOOOOOM!
It's what you will hear when Bleaty is near,
They call him The Sheep of Doom.

His Mum tried to raise him as best she could
But for her it was a shock
When this little sheep she could not keep
With the others in her flock.

Bleaty was a bit different, you see,
He had a mischievous streak.
He would completely, shear his whole family
While they were all asleep!

Bleaty's Mum didn't know what to do
And she reached the end of her tether,
When, for goodness sake, he put glue in the lake
So the ducks' feathers all stuck together!

Each farm animal signed a petition
And banished Bleaty to the barn
Where he sat all alone, in the dark, on his own,
And plotted revenge on the farm...

For weeks and months he stayed in there
And it became one happy farm.
The animals smiled with no sheep running wild
To ruin their peace and their calm.

Meanwhile, in the darkness, a
voice sneered:
"They're going to get such a
surprise!
Soon Bleaty KaBoom, The Sheep
of Doom,
Will pull the wool over their eyes!"

Quietly, in the dead of night,
Bleaty darted round the cow
pasture
Sprinting this way and that,
collecting cow pats,
So he could cause disaster!

He made a giant cow pat pile;
The smell was just appalling!
Then he blew them sky high, through the air they did fly!
On the animals they soon would be falling!

A SPLAT! here and a SPLOOSH!
there
But they weren't landing in the
right place!
It had all gone wrong and it
wasn't too long
Before Bleaty took one in the face!

"Plan B!" Bleaty bleated, wiping his brow
And holding a stick of dynamite.
To the hen-house he ran, "Let's see if I can
Give those dumb chickens a fright!"

He slid dynamite under a chicken
And cackled at what was to come.
"What better revenge then to blow
up some hens
By sticking a bomb up their
bum!?"

But the chickens noticed (just in
time!)
The dynamite between their legs.
The hens they scattered, while
Bleaty got splattered
By a shower of freshly-laid eggs!

Dripping with cow pats and hens' eggs
Bleaty yelled, "Plan C's the X Factor!
Let's see the reaction when I leap into action
And attack the farmer's new tractor!"

The Sheep of Doom grabbed a potato
And shoved it up the exhaust!
"When the farmer turns the key," he cackled with glee,
"It will cause much mayhem of course!!"

But when the tractor was started
No explosions…it just jolted the brake.
It shot down the track – hit Bleaty with a WHACK!
Catapulting him into the lake!

"That wasn't the plan!" Bleaty baaa-ed at the moon,
"This just isn't working!" he sighed.
"I've ended up soaked, covered with yolk
And smelling like a cow's backside!"

"Perhaps you need someone to talk to?"
Said an old cow, over the fence.
"If you get it all out, this anger and doubt,
It might make you feel not so tense."

So they talked and talked for hours,
Until the sun rose the next day.
Bleaty knew he'd been wrong, we should all get along
And destroying things isn't the way.

"The goats live their lives; the ducks do their thing,
Each animal has different needs.
I shouldn't cause harm, we all live on the farm,
Even though we are all different breeds."

"Some may have brown fur, some red feathers,
A few of us have a white fleece.
Let's not take, but give! Live and let live!
So says Bleaty Kaboom – Sheep of Peace!"

So from that day on, Bleaty changed his ways;
The black sheep of the family learned his lesson.
He's much happier now, thanks to his friend the cow
And a really good cow-ncelling session!

And that's the tale of Bleaty the sheep
Who's now stopped his raves and his rants.
Perfect he ain't, and I'm not saying he's a saint…
All I'm saying is 'Give sheep a chance.'

Octopus Jim

Octopus Jim is a popular guy,
He's got friend after friend,
But keeping in touch with all of them
Drives him round the bend.

The ocean is so very big,
With so many places to be
That with all the fishy friends Jim's got,
There's too many to see in the sea.

But now Jim stays in touch with his mates
No matter where he roams:
He took some birthday money he'd saved
And Jim bought eight i-phones!

Roger

There once was a lion called Roger.
At hunting he was rather poor.
Whilst trying to pounce on his dinner,
He'd miss and fall on the floor.

But his wife enjoyed eating antelope,
So, in order to please her,
Instead of hunting he's nip to the shop
And pick some up from the freezer.

Shoelace Boy

Shoelace boy met String Girl,
He thought that she was hot!
They went out for a while, settled down
Then thought they'd tie the knot.

Dog Nap

Dog lay in his basket.
His blanket kept him warm.
He'd had a tiring morning,
Digging up the lawn.

Doggy eyelids slowly drooped
Until he could not keep
His weary doggy body
From drifting off to sleep...

"I could be in the movies,"
Dog began to dream,
"And win lots of awards and things
For acting on the screen."

"I could be a secret agent,
Yeah, that would be nice!
Confronting Dr Tibbles
And his evil clockwork mice!"

"Or perhaps I'd be a huge monster
With an ultra-sonic ROOOOOAAAARRR!!
I'd crush entire cities
Under one gigantic paw!"

"Yes, this film would be the best,
An awesome action-thriller.
The people on the streets would yell,
"Look out! Here comes Dogzilla!"

"Or maybe aboard a great big boat
I could meet another dog.
We'd fall in lurve and sail the seas
(And maybe have a snog!)

"I'd squeeze her paw, the music would play,
Everything would be so nice.
Yep - this film would be unsinkable...
(If we just watched out for ice...)

"But then I could make my audience laugh
In a comedy role!
I'd cheekily chew on a rubber bone
And then fall in my bowl!"

"Then off to some very important awards
And how the crowd would cheer,
As I made my way to collect the trophy
For *The Funniest Dog of the Year!*"

"Or maybe I'd be on a planet far away
Yeah an alien I could be!
Just imagine a whole tribe of tall blue dogs
Coming at you in full on 3-D!"

"Yep I could be in the movies!
I could be an award winner!
But...it's so warm in my basket
And it's nearly time for dinner."

"Maybe tomorrow," Dog thought,
"Or maybe the day after that..."
Then flopped out of his basket
And went to chase a cat...

Get Your Room Clean!

My Mum's told me to get my room clean,
She says it's the biggest tip she's ever seen.
It's cluttered with books and comics and toys...
Hang on a second...what was that noise?

It isn't is it? No...it couldn't be!
I'll just ignore it 'cos I want my tea,
And I won't get any if this room's not tidy...
WAIT! YES IT IS!!!!

PIDEY! PIDEY! PIDEY!

Wang Foo the Kung Fu Shrew

I'll tell you a story that you won't believe,
But it happened just last week.
I was out in the park: it was just getting dark,
All the lights had come on in the street.

I strolled on the grass past a girl with her dog
And a boy climbing over the railing,
When shattering the hush – leaping out of a bush,
Came a huge cat, hissing and wailing...

On closer inspection I saw in its paws
What looked like a mouse or a rat.
They were kicking and fighting, scratching and biting,
"GET OFF HIM!" I yelled at the cat.

Both carried on scrapping, "Poor little thing!"
I thought, "I must intervene.
It's not right at all for a creature that small
To be picked on by something so mean!"

But when I looked closer that wasn't the case,
I'd got it the wrong way round!
The shrew was fighting back – he was on the attack!
And soon threw the cat to the ground!

It grabbed that poor pussy in its tiny paws
And spun him above his small head,
And despite his large size, if he'd not got nine lives,
I swear that cat would be dead!

Fur was flying everywhere,
As I looked on stunned and amazed!
With a THWAK! And a THOK! A WHACK! And a SOK!
The cat lay tongue out, both eyes glazed...

The rodent vanished into the night
Leaving a small calling card.
With great expectation I hoped for an explanation
As to why this shrew was so hard...

I slowly read the tiny words:
Is your cat evil? Here's what to do.
Don't hesitate – before it's too late,
Call WANG FOO THE KUNG FU SHREW!

Cats with attitude a speciality,
No job too big or too small.
Pedigree or shabby, Persian or Tabby,
Wang Foo will take them all!

I searched in the shadows to see where he went
But the light was starting to fade.
Out there in the night – filling felines with fright,
Is a rodent renegade.

It's since been whispered, behind closed doors,
That somewhere in these parts,
Is a hero for all, standing three inches tall,
A shrew trained in martial arts.

I've hung on to his number so I know what to do
If my cat is a problem at all.
If it causes mice harm or scratches my arm,
I'll give Wang Foo a call!

T.V.

There's nothing on the t.v., ever, ever, ever!
Just soaps and tacky talk shows
And forecasts on the weather.
Why don't people just switch off
If they don't like what they're seeing?
Go outside,
See the world
And be a human being!

Blah! Blah! Blah!

oooh... a 'talent' show...

Terence the Duck

Terence the duck was right out of luck
When it came to swimming too well.
As the people on land threw bread from their hand,
Terence would go through sheer hell.

His friends would see bread and leave him for dead,
With a whoosh and a splash they'd be there.
But try though he must to get one soggy crust,
His meal-times were getting quite rare.

So one day he thought "I know what must be bought,"
And went to the shop on the shore.
With a cheque that he wrote, he bought a speedboat,
And didn't go hungry anymore.

Ted's Bad Dream

If you give me a moment to set the scene,
I'll tell you the story of Ted's Bad Dream...

'Twas the night before Thursday
And all through the house
Not a creature was stirring
Except Ted the mouse.

He couldn't get thirty,
Never mind forty winks,
So he fluffed up his pillow
And lay back to think...

He thought of his bed,
And the wall over there.
"I'm safe and secure
And I don't have a care."

But then Ted thought harder,
Sat up and yawned,
And thought about life
Beyond his skirting-board...

His mind slowly wandered
To the friends that he had,
And how just lately
They looked kind of sad.

Take Kim the cow
And what she had to say:
"I stand in my field
And eat food all day."

"But every so often
I lean down for grass,
And spit out a can
Or a sharp piece of glass."

"While I'm eating my dinner
It makes my teeth judder.
Do you think I can eat it?
No way! Pull the udder!"

"We should look after the countryside,
And keep our eyes peeled.
Put cans and glass where they belong,
In a bin - not in my field!!"

Back in his mouse hole
Ted lay in bed
When his old friend the Fish
Swam into his head...

"I spend my days in this river,
Just swimming up and down.
It used to be a sparkling blue,
But now it's murky brown."

"There's a rusty bike, old car tyres,
Occasionally nuclear waste.
New things are dumped here every day,
I'm surprised I'm not fish paste."

"There was a time I had some friends,
With plants and life down here.
But that was before the poison and pain,
Back when the view was clear."

"When I think of what humans have done
It makes my scales quiver.
This isn't a bin to throw your junk in,
It's meant to be home - IT'S MY RIVER!!!"

Meanwhile in the hole
Ted lay in bed
And his old friend the Bird
Flew into his head...

"Way up here you would think
I'd be safe from man down there.
I'd fly through the sky, head held high,
Breathing clean, fresh air."

"I used to have not a care in the world,
Chirping my songs out loud.
Now the buildings and factories below
Send me thick, black cloud."

"Most of the time I can't see a thing,
Surrounded by pollution and smoke.
I've seen starlings cough, blackbirds gasp,
It's got beyond a joke."

"If only some of the factories would stop,
I'm sure the rest would follow.
It used to be so refreshing up here,
But now I can hardly swallow."

Meanwhile in his hole
Ted was sweating in bed
As his old pal the Dog
Leapt into his head...

"I love to scamper down the streets
And run about the place.
That is until a gust of wind
Blows paper in my face."

"It's great to go out for a walk
On my master's lead.
We walk for hours, never stop
(Only when I've peed)."

"Now, when I look down the street
What is it I see?
Pavements of litter, broken glass,
Walls of graffiti."

"My master often comments
How it all looks rather sad.
But if glass on the floor cut his paw,
He'd be barking mad!"

Back in the hole
Ted rolled out of bed,
Fell to the floor
And banged his head.

Ted woke up and looked around,
Then sat up with a start,
An aching feeling in his head,
A pounding in his heart.

The mouse stared out across the room,
The sweat started to stream.
He looked around, there was no sound,
"Thank goodness! Just a dream!"

He knew mankind would never get
Itself in such a state,
Killing creatures, polluting the earth,
Not knowing it's too late.

Ted thought to himself "Just in case,
There's something I must do."
He knelt by his bed and prayed in his head
That not all dreams come true...

Keith

Do you see over there
On that big green leaf?
It's a butterfly:
His name is Keith.
But he's not a real butterfly,
If you know what I mean.
As he doesn't like butter.
He prefers margarine.

Chips

I've just been to the chippy
And now I'm standing outside
Carrying two chips that are 8 feet tall
And just over 3 feet wide!

It's going to take me the rest of the week
To munch my way through these!
And all I said when I went in the shop
Was "Hello – Can I have large chips, please?"

Babies

There's a baby in a pram on the path over there,
Being pushed where she doesn't want to go.
She's zipped up in a coat and under a hat,
With only her eyes on show.

Doesn't she feel like just shouting, "STOP!!!
I don't want to go this way!
And how about letting me choose what I want
To wear when we're out for the day!"

Why doesn't she scream "LIBERATION!!!?
Stop pushing me around - I CAN WALK!"
Why don't they all rise and scream "LET US BE FREE!!!"

I s'pose it's 'cause babies can't talk.

There's Chicken Poo on my Egg!!

I'm with my Mum in the supermarket –
She's shopping, I'm being ignored.
We wander along aisles that go on for miles –
I'm very, very bored...

Down the cereal aisle we go,
Then up the aisle of cake.
We seem to have been here for days now –
My brain is starting to ache.

Then just as I'm losing my will to live,
With the trolleys to-ing and fro-ing,
I remember my favourite section,
The one place that keeps me going...

I push the trolley harder.
I run with my little legs
To the aisle of milk and butter,
But best of all...the eggs!

The excitement! The joy! The pleasure!
My smile is six feet wide!
As I pick up a carton of freshly laid eggs,
Pop the lid...and peer inside...

"Please let me be lucky!"
I screw my eyes tight and wish upon a star.
I feel like Charlie Bucket
Opening up a chocolate bar...

I check each eggshell carefully,
Lifting them up to see,
Will I be a winner
In this eggshell lottery?

Here we go, the last egg in the tray...
I pick it up...and grit my teeth...
And...WHAT!?! YES LOOK! I'VE FOUND SOME!
THERE'S A BIG CLUMP UNDERNEATH!!

THERE'S CHICKEN POO ON MY EGG!!
THERE'S CHICKEN POO ON MY EGG!!
PLEASE LOOK AT ME I BEG!!
THERE'S CHICKEN POO ON MY EGG!!

Sometimes it's brown, sometimes it's white,
Sometimes there's just a bit.
Occasionally you'll get really lucky
And a feather is stuck in it!

Sometimes it's just the one egg,
Now and again it's on two.
But it's the Holy Grail of dairy produce,
An egg with chicken poo!

Try it next time you're at the shops
To relieve your boredom and frustration.
Is there chicken poo on one of your eggs?
It's the craze that's sweeping the nation!

So, take it from me, someone who knows,
It'll make the dull shopping more fun!
If you can find an egg, with poo,
Fresh from a chicken's bum!

Pidey! Pidey! Pidey!

When you want to have a long hot bath
And you're standing on the rug,
Just starting to run the hot tap,
What's sitting near the plug?

Pidey! Pidey! Pidey!

If you're trying to get to sleep at night,
You've got that peepy feeling,
What's lurking in the darkness,
Hanging from the ceiling?

Pidey! Pidey! Pidey!

When you sit down to write a letter
To your bestest friend,
And pick up your most favourite pen,
What's dangling on the end??

Pidey! Pidey! Pidey!

You want to go out for a walk,
With your dog in the park,
But when you look inside your shoes,
What's hiding in the dark?

Pidey! Pidey! Pidey!

If you really want to read a book
And curl up in a chair.
When you find the page you're on,
What's running round in there?

PIDEY! PIDEY! PIDEY!

When you want to write a poem,
And you've got some great ideas,
You're sitting down – pen in
your hand,
What is it that appears?

PIDEY! PIDEY! PIDEY!!!!!!

AAAARRGGGHHHHHHHH!!!!!!!

Never Put Curry Up Your Nose

Never put curry up your nose,
You must fight your desire.
It's so flamin' hot when you blow your nose
You might just start a fire.

I Think There's a Monster Under My Bed!

I think there's a monster under my bed!
It started off just as a hunch,
But now I'm wondering if I should tell someone,
Before I end up its lunch!

There could be a monster under my bed!
Should I inform the authorities at once?
What if nothing's there and the army came out?
I could end up looking a dunce!

Is that a monster under my bed?
I'm about 88% certain.
I swear I just saw a large head pop out
And nibble a bit of the curtain.

I'm certain there's a monster under my bed!
The reason that I am now sure,
Is that when I got out to brush my teeth
There was a fifteen foot drop to the floor!

My Dog

My dog has only got one leg,
But apart from that - he's fine.
He can lick like other dogs,
And bark and growl and whine.
And if you scratch his tummy,
His tail will start to wag.
You just can't take him for a walk,
You take him for a drag.

Goldfish

I had a goldfish in a bowl,
I won him at the fair.
Today I went to feed him,
But my goldfish wasn't there!

He'd left me a goodbye note
Saying, "I can't stand it anymore.
I've taken my piano,
And gone on a world tour."

To be honest – I'm glad he's gone.
That fish was off the rails.
He kept me awake all night long,
Practising his scales.

Never Put Granny Up Your Nose

Never put Granny up your nose,
Of that, there is no doubt.
Imagine when you picked it
And her teeth came flying out!

Dinner

Do you ever stop and think
About the food that's on your plate?
Like, do they use real nans
In that naan bread you just ate?
And how about shepherd's pie,
Are there real shepherds inside?
Just think about the rioting sheep
About the countryside...
And what about toad-in-the-hole?
Is it really made from toads,
That are scraped up off the tarmac,
From Britain's major roads?
And then there are fish-fingers,
Is this really a dish
That's made from chopping digits off
Somebody's pet fish?
I think that we should all be told,
I really think we oughta,
And until I know all the facts

The Boy Who Loved Brussels

There was once this boy who loved Brussels sprouts;
I tell you – that's all he ate!
You'd not find beans or sausage or chips
Just Brussels on his plate.

If his mother made him sandwiches
What was between the bread?
Not cheese or spam, not eggs or ham,
Just juicy sprouts instead!

His parents took him to a posh restaurant,
A very fancy place.
But how embarrassed they both were
As he stuffed sprouts in his face!

Even Christmas dinner was different;
No giant turkey with veg on the side.
Just a little splash of gravy
On a Brussels sprout two metres wide!

Puddings and snacks were a little strange too;
The boy would sit watching the telly
Not devouring dessert of apple pie and cream
But a big bowl of sprout flavour jelly!

But this poem ends badly, I'm sorry to say,
For certain events came to pass.
For I'm sure that you know if you eat sprouts a lot
You'll build up a fair bit of gas...

The family was strolling back from the shops;
"My tummy hurts!" the young boy mumbled.
He dropped the shopping (which was mostly sprouts)
As his stomach gurgled and grumbled.

Then, with a huge BANG! his bottom exploded.
A great TTHHHRRRRPPPPP!! shot out of his cheeks!
He flew into space, the last time they saw his face,
Though the smell hung round for weeks...

"Good grief!" said his mother as the green smoke cleared,
"Our boy has gone! What a mess!"
"But look on the bright side," his father chipped in,
"Our Brussels sprout bill will be less!"

So next time you're told, "Eat your sprouts up!"
Read this rhyme out loud.
If they still say. "Eat a few!" then they just want you to
Disappear in a smelly green cloud!

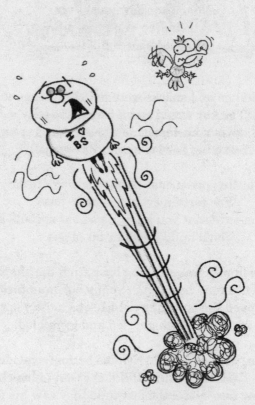

The Armadillo Under My Pillow

There's an armadillo under my pillow,
He's been there for a few days.
You might think he stops me from sleeping,
But I've got quite used to his ways.

If I'm tossing and turning and can't quite nod off,
No matter how hard I try,
The armadillo under my pillow
Will sing me a lullaby.

And the armadillo is amazing!
If I lose a sock whilst in bed
He'll search about and if he can't seek it out
He'll knit me a new one instead.

Sometimes in a morning if I can't quite get up,
And the alarm clock I just cannot hear,
He'll make sure I get out by opening his snout
And gently nibbling my ear.

Occasionally, if I'm reading a good book
But fall asleep before I'm done,
He'll switch off the light and tuck me in tight
And remember which page I was on.

I don't recommend one to everyone,
They're a bit of an acquired taste,
But if you eat cake in bed and armadillo's not fed
He'll hoover up all of the waste.

I'm not sure how he got there,
But my friends are all jealous, so,
While they all want to come round to see him,
I really don't want him to go.

I can only think of one drawback
About having him under my head:
No matter what I do, I can't train him to
Bring me my breakfast in bed!

Lucy Rabbit

Lucy was a rabbit,
She had so many kids.
She needed some time to herself
So guess what Lucy did?

She got a baby-sitter in,
Jumped into her car,
Then drove into town and sang all night
In a karaoke bar!

Lucy was a rabbit
With one big family.
I think that since the last verse
It's gone up to twenty-three!

She felt she couldn't cope again,
She needed time off, so,
Once more she got a sitter in
And went to play Bingo!

Lucy was a rabbit,
I think you know the rest,
But this time it's not Lucy
But her kids that are all stressed.

"Mum, we never see you much!
You disappear for hours!"
So that week-end she took them all
On a trip to Alton Towers.

Arma Feelin' Chilly!

On a dark and chilly winter's night
When I can see my breath in the air,
And I just can't get snuggly in my bed
I'm glad Armadillo is there.

He'll do ten laps around my room
'Til he's sweating from the heat.
Then I'll use him as a hot-water bottle
To pop under the sheet!

My Hamster

My hamster's only got one eye
In the middle of his head.
He just sits there and stares at me
As I get ready for bed.

And when I walk around my room
I somehow still can feel,
His hamster eye fixed right on me
Even though he's on his wheel.

At night-time when all proper pets
Towards sleep should be heading,
I still can see his beady eye
Peeping through his bedding.

I think next time I get one
I'll make sure that mum buys
One that's a little nicer
And has got both of its eyes!

Rigor Mortis in my Tortoise

My tortoise has rigor mortis.
I know they don't move a lot.
But mine now doesn't move at all:
Rigor mortis he has got.
I thought he was slow before
But now he won't walk, drink or eat.
Yep – my tortoise has rigor mortis.
I wonder if I kept the receipt?

Armadillo Walkies

I took my armadillo down to the park
Where he caused a bit of a stir.
Most of the people who stopped to look
Thought it was a dog with no fur.

A man said, "It looks like a tortoise!"
A lady laughed, "What a strange pet!"
But keep your dogs and cats, your hamsters and rats,
An armadillo's the best you can get!

After a run on the grass we went home.
My pet was real tired, so
As his eyes slowly shut, I quietly put
The pillow under my armadillo!

Greyhounds I Have Known

It was a cosy Sunday afternoon
In the home of Grandpa Hare.
He sat under an old blanket,
In his rocking chair.

The elderly hare was worn and grey,
One of his ears was missing,
But he felt young again when the grandkids came round
To hear Grandpa reminiscing...

They'd sit in a circle surrounding his chair
And hang on every word,
Of tales of life in days gone by,
Stories they'd never heard.

You see Grandpa Hare wasn't normal,
You wouldn't know to look at his face.
He was, in fact, a mechanical hare.
The sort that greyhounds chase.

Grandpa had worked for many a year,
We're talking a while back,
As packs of dogs would follow him,
Round the local greyhound track.

He'd been the best at what he did,
Ran circuits in record time,
And no greyhound EVER beat Grandpa Hare
In crossing the finishing line.

"Tell us again!" piped up one tiny hare,
"Oh Grandpa, we'd all love to hear
Of some of the famous greyhounds
That you've beaten in your career!!"

Grandpa sat back, feeling warm and proud,
Like a king upon his throne.
"Gather round little ones and I'll tell you the names
Of the greyhounds I have known..."

"Fat Jenny, Slim William, Lanky Montell,
'Round' Martha and Old Whiskered Tim.
Muzzled Pauline, Sleek Johnny, Slick Simon,
Bulbous-Eyed Eric, Lithe Jim."

"Ribby George, 'Tubby' Cedric, Leggy Katherine,
Lean Kenneth, Small-Snouted Sam.
Slender James, Small-Eared Ethel, 'Fat' Matthew
And the 50-to-1 shot, 'Big' Pam."

"There was Gaunt Features Graham and Slender Kate,
A spindly dog that they called Bones.
Identical twins, 'Porky' Pat and Pat 'Porky',
And Mr. Rodney 'the whippet' Jones."

"Don't forget Swift Yvonne and Tiny Feet Jan,
Boney Bill and Whirlwind Greg.
And most bizarrely I remember this race
With a dog that had only one leg."

"Pot-Bellied Benji, Two-Headed Dave,
Who was tested for steroids, I heard,
And a greyhound they told me was
owned by the Queen
Called Sir Cecil Smythe-Farquar the Third."

"Lightening Neil, who, whenever he ran,
Got record times for the course.
And Gigantic Greg, who after inspection,
Turned out to be a small horse."

"Yes! I raced them all and beat them!
I really was the best!
But excuse me; it's time for my afternoon nap,
Even mechanical hares need their rest..."

Never Put Lawn-Mowers
Up Your Nose

Never put lawn-mowers up your nose,
Not even for a dare.
You'll have to find some other way
To trim your nasal hair.

Simon

Simon was a worker ant,
He worked and worked all day.
Lifting stones twice his height
With never time to play.

One morning Simon woke and thought,
"I don't fancy work today."
So he rang in sick and took his wife
On a skiing holiday.

Henry

Henry was a caterpillar,
The nicest you could meet,
He had a long, green body
And lots of tiny feet.

But although his body was hairy,
I'm afraid it must be told,
He had no hair upon his head.
He was completely bald!

Henry tried so many ways
To hide his lack of hair:
A scarf, a hat - forget all that!
His scalp was still threadbare.

Henry knew what must be done
So he took a trip one day,
Withdraw his savings from the bank
And bought a big toupee.

Centipedes swooned and fleas fainted,
Henry's now a lady-killer!
He's known wood-wide as the wonderful
Wiggy, wiggly caterpillar!

The Dancing Ladybird

There I was lying on the settee
Just the other day,
When an insect flew in my window
And stood next to where I lay.

It turned out to be a ladybird.
And one that could really move!
Her six legs started dancing –
That bug was in the grooooove!

She danced upon the tables,
She danced upon the chairs,
She danced into the hallway
And danced right up the stairs.

But the ladybird kept falling over,
Her dancing wasn't quite right.
"I'll sort my steps out!" the ladybird said,
And to the bathroom took flight.

I ran into the bathroom after her
And it all fell into place –
There she was upon the sink,
A smile upon her face!

You see she'd found her style and moves,
Even though it sounds absurd,
The insect that flew in my window was
A tap-dancing ladybird!

Fly Guy

Of all the super heroes,
Fly Guy is the worst.
His powers include landing on food
And buzzing round your head 'til you curse.

And this half-man/half-fly crusader
Is easy to defeat.
You don't need Kryptonite – a newspaper rolled tight
Will knock him out a treat!

The Great Stupeedo

I have to tell you all about
The worst magician I've ever seen.
He could saw a woman in two
But the mess left behind was obscene!

There were no white rabbits in his hat,
Just a piece of fluff.
And the only thing he could make disappear
Was his audience in a huff!

Goldfish World Tour 2010

I was wandering down the street one day,
And I passed a huge concert hall.
There outside I saw a poster,
Pasted to the wall.

The poster read '7-30 TONIGHT,
THE PERFORMER WHO'S ALL THE RAGE!"
And there was a picture of my pet fish,
Playing live on stage.

The very same fish who'd deserted his bowl,
The fish who was off the rails.
But it seemed him and his piano were now
Having mega record sales!

It seems everyone adores his songs,
No matter what he croons!
And my ex-pet is the biggest-selling fish
To ever appear on i-tunes!

I bought a ticket and went along
To the fish's Grand World Tour.
The lights went out, the crowd erupted,
And I couldn't believe what I saw...

There was the fish at the piano,
He sat there singing and playing.
The crowds loved him, they clapped along,

Other times they were singing and swaying.
I was amazed at how good he'd got,
I'm surprised he's not made it big sooner.
He sang and played like no fish before
And never hit a note out of tuna.

He rocked the joint and they loved him so much,
Be it father, son, mother or daughter.
He'd found his plaice! He was a Rock Cod!
Never looking like a fish out of water!

I thought for a moment, looking into the crowd,
My fish had spotted my face.
It was just before he started a song called
'Chris White's a Disgrace'.

After the concert everyone left
And it really, really hurt
To hear the crowds saying how good he was,
And buying their fish tour t-shirt.

I tried to get backstage to see him
But security thought me a nutter.
I was yelling "BUT I WAS HIS OWNER!!"
But they still threw me into the gutter…

I really, really hate that fish,
But I know he also dislikes me.
I think I'll move on and buy a new one,
There's plenty more fish in the sea

The Man on the Train

There's a man that sits on the train with me
Who has a black brief-case.
He sits in the same seat everyday,
And has an evil face.

He often glances at me
And his eyes burn into mine.
You can sometimes hear him mumbling
That the train is not on time.

As I sit there in a morning
Thoughts always come to me.
Just what exactly is within
The briefcase on his knee?

On a Monday it's maybe a monster,
With horns and a mouth like a funnel,
That he uses to suck up small children
Whenever we go through a tunnel.

On a Tuesday I think it's a tentacle
That unravels itself for a mile,
Then grabs the ticket conductor's leg
And drags him down the aisle.

On Wednesday I wonder if it is a wolf
That leaps out of the case with a wail!
It slobbers on the man next to me,
Then bites a hole in his *Daily Mail*!

On Thursday I'm thinking that there is a
thing
That came from outer space.
It followed a lady into the loo
And she came out with spots on her face.

On Friday I fear that a few hundred
fish
Spill out onto the floor,
And they make such a smell on the
platform outside
When the train opens its door.

(I'm afraid I can't tell you if the weekend's the same,
Because on Saturday and Sunday I don't get the train...)

I think the man is suspicious
As he keeps glaring at me,
And I think that he knows that I think in his case,
Is something I'm not meant to see...

But I'm sure it's only papers and files
That the brief-case holds inside.
But I think I prefer my version of things,
It makes for a less boring ride!

Thoughts on my Rubber Duck

I'm lying in the bathtub,
There's isn't much to do.
I've bathed my bits, washed my armpits,
My hair's had a shampoo.

I could lie here thinking happy thoughts.
Or I could think of my troubles.
When – here's some luck! Here comes my duck,
Floating through the bubbles.

You realise I don't mean a real one?
No – that would be too fantastic!
It's one that for a laugh, you put in your bath,
And is made out of bright yellow plastic.

He swims length after length of my bath.
How many? Don't know – I've forgotten.
But he's here every week with a smile on his beak,
And 'Made in Taiwan' on his bottom.

I've had my duck friend since I was a boy,
We've been through thick and thin.
During my ups and downs he's always been around,
But my duck won't sink – just swim.

I wonder sometimes what he's thinking.
Does he think that I'm quite strange?
It just can't be read what's in his yellow head –
As his expression doesn't change.

I've never given him a name.
He is, I'm not sure, just how old.
But I do know there's no doubt I should be getting out,
As my bathwater's getting quite cold!

The Big, Big Guinea Pig

My guinea pig won't stop eating,
That's all he seems to do.
I used to feed it twice a day
But now it's twenty-two!

He's growing too big for his cage
And I think that very soon,
At the rate my guinea pig's growing
He'll take up all my room.

I'll have to move my bed out
And all my books and toys.
Imagine what a smell there'd be
And just think of the noise.

I'd have to move him to the yard
If he grew that big.
But he could scare burglars away,
Yeah! My own guard guinea pig!!

And if he started growing
To an even bigger size,
I'd need a Ferris wheel
To give him exercise.

But imagine how my friends would stare
And how they'd make a fuss,
When I came to school on my huge pet
Instead of on the bus.

I hope he doesn't get much bigger,
As I think without a doubt,
It would be the worst thing in the world
To clean a giant guinea pig out!!

Tadpole

I caught a tadpole in a pond
And put him in a jar.
I wasn't sure what to feed him on
So I gave him a chocolate bar.

But that was a bad idea;
He ate and ate and ate
One chocolate bar after another –
Now my tadpole's a tad overweight.

So I bought him a fitness DVD
Which he watches to keep fit and train.
Now he's back to his old tadpole self;
You could say he feels spawn again!

Sisqo the Shrimp

Sisqo the shrimp was off to the gym
With his good pal Pedro the prawn.
They thought they would go and lift a few weights
And try to build their fishy brawn.

But when they got there they stood out a mile,
And got into one or two tussles.
They weren't in the swim and didn't blend in
As the gym was packed full of mussels!

Bitey: The Vampire Bites Back

Blow your sniffling nostrils,
And wipe your teary eye
For it seems the veggie vampire,
Didn't really die!

Bitey walks amongst us!
He's alive for goodness' sake!
Whoever said he's dead's dead wrong,
The whole thing one missed steak!

The tubby meat-free vampire
For a while there looked doomed,
But you know how some exaggerate
A tiny little wound.

And despite his awkward accident,
Bitey looks alright:
His hair slicked back, his eyes blood-shot,
His skin a deathly white.

"I think I'm going to be ok,
But just so there's no doubt,
I'll visit the doctor's surgery
So he can check me out."

Although he didn't like going
Bitey thought, "Be brave!
It's not everyday you die,
Then end up rising from the grave."

Bitey sat in the waiting room,
Dreaming of crackers and cheese,
But his thoughts of food were burst – when the nurse,
Stuck her head in and yelled "NECKS PLEASE!!"

"Good evening," said a hairy thing,
"It's nice to have you back."
The thing was Bitey's doctor,
Last name Hill, first name Jack.

Dr. Hill took Bitey's pulse,
Just like yours or mine.
But vampires don't have one,
So that was a waste of time.

Then, in went a thermometer,
Which came out freezing cold.
(You don't have a lot of body heat
When you're over three centuries old!)

Next, Bitey was placed on the scales,
They said he was overweight –
(That must be all the veggie burgers
And mushroom pies he ate!)

And finally, a blood test,
Which Bitey found quite sore.
Until he glimpsed a drop of blood
And passed out on the floor.

Summing up, the doctor said,
"There's nothing wrong with you!
You're in quite good condition
For a man of three hundred and two!"

So Bitey left the surgery
Feeling quite upbeat,
And the veggie vampire's thoughts soon turned
To having a bite to eat.

"Some celebratory slap-up nosh!"
The vampire did squeal.
"A pasta bake, some lentil soup,
A nice Quorn ready meal!"

Under cover of moonlight
To a restaurant he did trot,
The waiter gave Bitey a menu,
Bitey said "Fangs a lot!"

He carefully perused the options,
Deciding what to eat,
Checking each dish carefully
To be sure it wasn't meat.

But, I'm afraid; Bitey's meal didn't
go well
In fact…he ended up dead!
It's not wise for a veggie vampire
To have a starter of garlic bread…

Itchy the Witch

The weirdest witch I ever met
Was Itchy the witch, for sure!
She couldn't cast spells, her black cat smells,
And her evil potions were poor.

So she used her big, black cauldron
Not for brews or curses of old,
But to boil batches of mushroom soup
For the homeless when it gets cold.

Frankenhamster

He died one tragic winter's night;
I didn't have a clue
That my hamster's final resting place
Would be under my Auntie's shoe.

They said he'd never live again,
That my experiments were frightening.
But they reckoned without my toaster
And a well-placed bolt of lightening.

I shoved my hamster in the slot for bread,
The lightning struck the appliance
And he popped out, lightly toasted but ALIVE!!
It's a wonder of modern science!

Sure, he looks a little odd.
He's whiffy, but what the heck!
He's my very own Frankenhamster
With a bolt through his furry neck.

He walks around like he did before,
Though sometimes he's splutterin' and coughin'
You wouldn't really know he's dead
Except sometimes bits drop off him.

But I'll never need to feed him again!
So I think, you will discover,
As long as I charge him up overnight
It's cheaper than buying another!

My Cat Needs Glasses

I think my cat needs glasses,
As when he's had a nap
He jumps out of his basket
And heads for his cat flap,
But instead of going through it,
His head will THWACK! the door,
And when I get home, there's my cat,
Unconscious on the floor.

My Rabbit

My rabbit likes to wear make-up,
I think it is a pity
How the other rabbits make fun of him
As I think he looks quite pretty!

He's so fashion conscious
There's a mirror in his hutch!
Now he wants me to take him to get his ears pierced
But I think that'll cost way too much.

Never Put Monkeys Up Your Nose

Never put monkeys up your nose;
It's not that they will harm us
It's just that when you take a deep breath
You'll smell nothing but bananas.

The Strangest Dream

I had the strangest dream last night,
It didn't make sense at all.
I dreamt I had a guinea pig
And it was ten feet tall.

And as I took it for a walk,
People would stop and stare.
I guess a ten-foot guinea pig
Is probably quite rare.

Then as we were out strolling
I met a fluffy rabbit.
She wouldn't stop warbling Karaoke
(A most annoying habit.)

She told me, whilst still singing,
To go and catch a bus.
So I did as I was told to do
Without making a fuss.

I waited – soon the bus came,
I smiled and paid my fare,
But I had trouble believing
Who else was sat in there.

A baby, with a huge quiff,
Sat talking to his father.
Then look! A slug and a centipede
Both in a balaclava.

A hamster with just one eye,
A bear that looked insane,
A man with a brief-case mumbling how
He usually gets the train.

A ferret with a guitar,
A monkey with plenty to eat,
And I'm sure I saw a Pidey
Run under the driver's seat!

Oh yes! About the driver,
The driver was a duck,
But one who'd passed his driving test
So there's a bit of luck.

He had a hat upon his head,
A waistcoat on his back,
And when the bus ran over bumps
He'd flip in the air and quack!

The bus sped through the countryside
And off into the night.
Passing a tooth shaped castle
All shiny and white.

Eventually the bus stopped.
I got out in front of a shop.
My mouth was getting quite dry,
So I thought I'd buy some pop.

The shopkeeper was a tiny mouse,
Peering over the till.
He stared at me as I walked in,
His voice was high and shrill...

"Welcome to my humble shop.
What would you like to buy?
Maybe a coffee and sugar baguette
Or a nice slice of wool pie?"

"Or a drink of tepid bath water?
A cake filled with dandruff?
Or how about a sandwich filled
With belly button fluff?"

"Just this can of cola, thanks.
How much do I owe?"
I gave the mouse one hundred pounds
And quickly turned to go.

"THAT'S NOT ENOUGH!!" the mouse roared.
I had a real bad feeling –
As the mouse got angry he started to grow
'Til his ears were touching the ceiling!

I ran out into the street again.
"I must get away, but to where?"
I didn't want to go back in the shop
As the service was lousy in there.

The mouse, meanwhile, kept on growing.
He burst right through the shop wall.
I took off down the High Street

But I couldn't run at all.The more I tried to speed away
The slower I seemed to get.
The mouse was right behind me,
Getting angrier I bet!

Then, screeching round the corner,
Came a taxi, big and black.
The driver rolled down the window and squeaked,
"Quick matey – jump in the back!"

The driver was a clockwork mouse
Who sensed I was in trouble,
"Looks like you've dreamed enough tonight.
Wakey Town on the double!!"

The taxi roared towards Wakey Town,
The driver put the pedal to the floor,
And as he looked in the rear view mirror
He couldn't believe what he saw...

The mouse from the shop was in pursuit!
By now it had grown *really* big!
I was sweating with fear, but then who should appear?
It's my giant guinea pig!

The mouse turned to scamper away
When he heard my guinea's mighty squeak!
He got the mouse on the run by nibbling his bum
So he couldn't sit down for a week!

The taxi meter clicked round to 6-30
And then it started to beep,
When I realised it was my alarm clock,
And that I was no longer asleep.

"What a strange dream." I wearily thought.
"I must write down that one..."
So I got up there and then, grabbed a pen,
And that's exactly what I've just done.

I strolled from my bed, the dream in my head,
And as if that wasn't bad enough,
As I stretched and yawned, a thought suddenly dawned,
"Why's my belly-button full of fluff?!?!?"

Something Smelly

There's something smelly in the fridge,
Is it cheese or some other fare?
No, I'm afraid the dog is dead,
So I went and stuffed him in there!!

Ostrich Man

One superhero you don't hear about
Is the amazing Ostrich Man.
I don't think he'll ever save the world
But he does the best that he can.

His neck is so long he can see round corners.
He can lay super eggs all the time.
And using his feathers he'll tickle the suspect
Until they admit to the crime!

But, unlike Superman, he can't even fly!
He just tends to run around.
And if he ever sees bad trouble coming
He'll stick his head in the ground!

Wang Foo 2: Re-enter the Shrew

I'm gonna tell you a story that you won't believe,
But it happened the other day.
I'd gone round to see Gran, I do when I can,
As it's not too far out of my way.

We sat in the front room having a chat
And drinking hot tea from a mug,
When in through the door, trotting over the floor,
Came a huge cat that sat on the rug.

Gran chirped, "This is my cat Tiger,
He's the sweetest cat you'll ever see!"
I reached to stroke his head, but what happened instead,
Is that Tiger reached out and scratched me!

"He's only playing!" my Gran said,
"That means he likes you – no doubt!"
But I wasn't so sure, my arm was quite sore
Where his claws had suddenly lashed out.

But then I looked closer at Tiger's large mouth
And saw, hanging out of his jaws,
Swinging by its tail, was a mouse, old and frail,
That Tiger would prod with his paws.

"Isn't he clever?" beamed Granny,
"Tiger has caught his own supper!"
But I thought it unfair that the mouse should be there,
As Gran went to brew a fresh cuppa.

As she hobbled away with the empty mugs
Tiger dropped the mouse and went too.
The mouse lay there twitchin' as they went to the kitchen
And I wished there was something I could do.

The poor little creature looked on its last legs.
It was bruised, battered and scarred.
Then, quick as a blur, it reached into its fur,
And brought out a small calling card!

The mouse dragged itself 'cross the carpet
Towards my Gran's telephone.
With its last mousey breath (just before mousey death),
It dialled, then collapsed with a moan...

A few minutes passed, Granny and cat returned
With a tray of tea and Hob Nobs.
Gran put down the tray, Tiger picked up his prey,
Then Granny nipped off to do jobs...

What happened next was amazing:
The cat threw the mouse in the air,
Opened his mouth wide for the mouse to drop inside –
I looked on in horror and despair...

Then suddenly, darting through the living room,
And catching the mouse en-route,
Came a small, furry ball standing 3 inches tall
Wearing a white karate suit!

It was Wang Foo the Kung Fu Shrew!
The first mammal of martial arts!
When mice are gripped with fear – Wang Foo will appear!
And fur's gonna fly when he starts!

Wang Foo took the mouse to the skirting board
And placed him inside a mouse hole.
With Tiger in sight, he pulled his black-belt tight
And yelled, "C'mon Pussy, let's wok and roll!"

They lunged at each other like you've never seen!
They went at it like thunder and lightning.
Paw against paw on the living room floor.
A cat and shrew kung fu fighting!

The cat whacked the shrew; the shrew struck the cat –
They were locked in a martial arts fix.
The cat looked like winning, 'til Wang Foo sent him spinning
With a flurry of chop shrewy kicks!

The cat then struck back, teeth biting, fur flying,
It was hard to tell who was more able.
Then, with a mighty roar, Tiger jabbed out a paw
Knocking Wang Foo under the table.

The shrew lay behind a table leg,
Dazed and not sure what to do;
The cat was ready to kill, Wang Foo lay very still –
It was crouching Tiger, hidden shrew.

With the cat primed to pounce, Wang Foo lay there.
Was he dazed or in a deep trance?
Could he be meditating? Just lying there waiting?
Would he soon rise in a kung fu stance?

Sure enough, up he leapt with an almighty squeeeeeeak!
Tiger gulped and looked very afraid,
Then was struck on the nose and upwards he rose
Towards my Grandma's light shade...

Granny returned to the room and asked,
"Are you alright? I thought I heard squealing!"
She gasped in disbelief, spitting out her false teeth,
"Why's my pet cat hanging from the ceiling?!?"

I didn't tell Granny what happened to Tiger,
She wouldn't believe me, I think.
But she saw the old mouse strolling out of her house,
Turn and give me a smile and a wink.

The kung fu shrew had vanished once more,
And that's nearly the end of my story.
Another bad cat has felt, the wrath of his black-belt
And tasted the furry fists of fury!

And Tiger the cat is much nicer now,
He's a far, far friendlier beast.
He's cuddly and nice, respects voles and mice
And especially shrews from the Far East.

Bread Boy

Bread Boy met Crumpet girl;
Their relationship couldn't fail.
They got married one summer's day
Before the romance went stale.

But their perfect day was ruined
When they reached the reception room:
The guests all stood and said, "Three Cheers!"
Then toasted the bride and groom.

Elephant John

There was once an elephant called John,
The wrinkliest creature ever seen!
He'd had them for years – round his eyes, round his ears,
Oh! To be smooth was his dream!

So he took a trip to the chemist
As he had a clever notion.
He grabbed off the shelf, a gift for himself:
A jar of anti-wrinkle lotion.

Now he sticks his trunk in the jar twice a day
And slaps it on, slippin' and sloppin',
Then rubs it in good, and I tell you – he should!
Oooh! It's taken ten years off him!

Dragon for Hire

If I said I knew of a dragon,
Who was friendly and not at all bad.
If I told you I knew of a dragon,
Would you tell me that I was quite mad?

I'll do my best to tell you his story:
I think he was short and quite podgy,
Some of my memories are sketchy you see,
And some of my rhyming is dodgy.

I know he was born all alone in the world,
Not hatched into titles or wealth.
His mother and father were nowhere around,
So he had to look after himself.

As the dragon thought of his purpose in life,
And down what path he'd be led,
He let out a cough, flames shot from his jaws,
And burnt down a nearby cowshed!

"HOLY SMOKE!!" the dragon screamed,
"Where did that come from?"
Then realised he'd been given a gift,
And a very useful one...

"I now know what I must do:
Go forth and create fire!
People will flock from miles around
When they see *Dragon for Hire...*"

So the dragon set off walking,
To see what jobs he could find.
Something quite glamorous, well-paid
and well-loved
Were the things he had in mind.

He'd not been walking for too long,
When he came across a town,
And running towards him was a man,
Waving a sausage up and down!

The man said, "I've got all my family round,
But I don't know what I'm gonna do!
They're sat in my garden with empty stomachs and plates,
'Cause I can't light my barbecue!"

"Aha!" thought the dragon.
"Here's my big chance!"
He stood, legs astride, and took aim...
Not only did the barbie light up,
The whole garden went up in flames!

"STOP THAT DRAGON!" Aunt Nelly yells.
"Call the cops!!" Cousin Colin blabs,
But the dragon had scampered down the street
In a shower of burning kebabs...

"Not to worry!" The dragon thought,
"I'll get it right next time.
There must be someone that can use
This red hot gift of mine!"

"Hey! Over here!" the cry came
And the dragon spun around.
He saw two men under a balloon
That couldn't get off the ground.

"We're trying to get this thing moving,
We want to be up there.
You wouldn't be a darling, would you,
And lend us your hot air?"

Dragon stepped into the basket
And blew with all his might.
An orange flame warmed the air,
The balloon slowly took flight...

Up they went into the sky,
Slowly getting higher.
Everything was going well until...
The balloon went and caught fire!!

There was much plummeting and
shouting.
Dragon knew he'd made a mistake
When they yelled, "Get lost Scaly!
You're useless!"
From the middle of a lake.

Undeterred, the dragon strolled on,
Feeling quite alone,
When a few yards down the street he saw
A frozen old folk's home.

"Our boiler is broken," an old man said.
"We sit down to have a natter,
But it's so cold in there – I swear,
If we had teeth, they'd chatter!"

The dragon surveyed the boiler
And it looked ever so old.
But he just couldn't leave the people here,
To play dominoes in the cold.

He took a pipe into his mouth,
Held it with a paw,
And heat soared through the frosted pipes.
The room began to thaw...

"One more puff should do it!"
The old folks all cried, "NO!!
The boiler's so old, if you heat it some more
The whole place is gonna blow!!"

"Too late!" shouted someone…then there was a BOOOOM!
That shattered the double glazing.
Everywhere you looked cardigans were cooked,
And war blazers were blazing.

"GET OUT!!" cried the old folks, catching their breath,
"You're no use to anyone!"
As walking sticks waved and zimmer frames were flung,
In a puff of smoke…he was gone…

And that's how I remember the story,
Of a dragon that must be admired,
For persisting to share his fire with the world,
Even though it kept getting him fired.

And that is why the last dragon died out,
There was nothing for him to do.
So if you have a talent, make sure that it's used,
Or the same thing may happen to you!

Andrea the Dolphin

The dolphins swam and leapt and dived
In the deep blue sea.
Their eyes sparkled in the sunshine,
The most beautiful creatures there could be.

BUT LOOK! Just behind that graceful gang
You'll see a dolphin on her own.
It's Andrea the dolphin,
She's swimming all alone...

Andrea, you see, isn't graceful,
She can't swim too well, I think.
She splashes and crashes and can't keep up.
She doesn't swim...just sinks.

But dolphins are very intelligent
And Andrea had a good notion:
She slowly floated to the shop on the shore
Where you buy beach balls and suntan lotion.

Now Andrea the dolphin has a smile on her face,
Because with the others she swims!
She's a more graceful thing, with her big rubber ring,
And a pair of armbands on her fins!!

Abb.

The world is such a crazy place,
Full of the strange and absurd.
Like why is abbreviation,
Such a very long word?

Fang

In a place, in the woods, in the dark, in a cave,
Is a place where the bats all hang.
Most of them are vampire bats,
But not the one called Fang.

Every night at 12 o'clock
You can hear a thousand wings,
Taking little furry bats
To dine on living things.

The vampire bats go out at night,
To suck on cows, moths or flies.
Fang sits alone, nibbling a plum,
Then just breaks down and cries.

The other bats don't get him,
They won't give him a break.
Fang, you see, is a fruit bat,
But they call him a fruit cake.

He doesn't fancy sucking blood
Like that bloodthirsty lot.
Fang prefers some nuts or dates,
Maybe a nice kumquat!

But more than that, at the end of the night,
When he is cold and tired,
Fang longs for someone to care for him,
To be loved and desired.

Someone who understands him.
Someone to share his pain.
So off he flapped into the night,
Flitting through the rain.

And who knows where he got to?
Did he find someone to care?
Who can tell, but you know what they say –
There's someone for everyone out there...

Pumpkin

Once upon a time there was a pumpkin
Who was large and orange and round.
She was born in the pumpkin patch just up the road
And grew up from the ground.

She spent her days looking towards
Her very first Halloween.
It was a special time for pumpkins, she'd heard,
The best there'd ever been.

She concentrated on getting juicy and big
So she would look her best.
On October 1st she was sent to the shops,
Just like all the rest.

She sat in the shop, was picked up and squeezed,
Until somebody bought her.
A man took her home for a Halloween treat
For Florence, his small daughter.

Halloween came – pumpkin sat in the window
Of her new owners' old home.
She smiled a jagged pumpkin smile,
A vegetable all alone...

From the window she watched as the sun went down,
Her pumpkin heart excitedly beating.
What scenes she saw: people dressed up!
Young children trick or treating!

She started to wonder, as the moon came up,
What wonderful things were in store?
What would fill her head? What feelings inside
To treasure forever more?

But please don't expect a happy ending
For there's not one, it has to be said.
Her insides were scooped out to make pumpkin pie
And a candle was shoved in her head.

Carol

Carol the worm had no friends I'm afraid,
Her life was one long toil.
She longed for another to burrow along
And join her in the soil.

Days turned to weeks, turned to months, turned to years,
And Carol was still alone.
No other worms came calling
At her quiet underground home.

So one day Carol took action and cried,
"I think that I have earned
My right to be happy – not miserable!
Today, this worm has turned!"

Carol's a different worm these days,
She's got loads of friends now;
She gets to speak with them everyday,
Let me tell you how...

Carol bought a PC,
And all the friends she's met
Are the product of being the world's first worm
To be on the Internet!

Donkeys

The donkeys stand in their green, grassy field
Under the pale blue sky.
One may lean his head over the gate
To watch the world go by...

From his field he can view people like me and you,
Living our lives day by day,
And sometimes what he sees makes him fall to his knees,
And let out a long, forlorn bray.

Look! Can you see? Past the hedge, past the tree,
The by-pass snaking through the Dales,
Where hundreds of cars locked bumper to bumper
Crawl along like big metal snails.

Inside each car sit all kinds of folk
Of different size and age,
But with one thing in common – they're hot, mad and lost
And all struck down with road rage.

Dad swears it's this junction – Mum says that it's not!
And, "How many sweets can we have?!"
Crying babies ignored, kids complaining they're bored,
Whilst Granny talks to the Sat-Nav.

Then look down the street – see a couple of people
Out for a stroll in the sun.
They're enjoying a drink from a bottle of pop,
One's chewing some bubble gum.

But when they have finished do they locate a bin?
No, I'll tell you what that couple do:
Lob the bottle in a field – drop the gum on the ground
To lie in wait for a shoe.

On the brow of the hill sits a factory
Churning out smoke day and night,
Coughing up clouds of chemicals
That smother the morning sunlight.

So, as the light disappears and the day becomes cold
And the couple row over a jumper,
Their shouts are drowned out by the curses and yells
Of the drivers locked bumper to bumper...

And the smoke from their exhausts builds up and up
'Til it slowly spirals high,
Where it mingles and mixes with the factory clouds
In a grey blanket covering the sky.

And all this time the donkeys stand in their field
Just watching, not making a fuss,
And it all makes you wonder – which ones are the donkeys,
Is it them, or is it us?

Chopsy the Chubby Chihuahua

Look who's coming down the street,
Belly dragging on the ground:
It's Chopsy the Chubby Chihuahua!
The podgiest doggy around!

He's not very big height-wise,
But round his waist instead.
He's yappy but happy, has four little legs
And two big bug-eyes in his head.

Don't expect to see him chasing cats,
A greyhound he is not!
Chopsy's so chubby, as soon as he runs,
He collapses on the spot.

Some dogs have a little coat
To warm their doggy bits.
Not Chopsy – his owners have tried everywhere
But can't find one that fits.

Not that he really needs one.
Because of his shapely form,
Instead of shivering like other small doggies,
His layers of fat keep him warm.

He lies in his extra-large basket
And never will be thin,
'Cos he never exercises
And eats dog food tin after tin.

Because he eats so much doggy dinner
His bowel movements are super!
His owners have had to have specially made
An industrial strength pooper-scooper!

Yep! There goes little Chopsy.
Waddling at one mile an hour.
You never did see, a dog so portly
As Chopsy the Chubby Chihuahua!

Quincy O'Hara
the Police Force Koala

It was Australia that tried it first
But it never quite caught on here.
Police dogs? YES! Police horse? OF COURSE!
A police koala? Oh dear...

It seemed like a great idea at first;
They had a little uniform made.
The word was put out on the streets
"The cop koala must be obeyed."

They thought if someone had robbed a bank
And hidden up a tree,
Quincy Koala would climb up like a shot
And arrest him easily.

But things started going wrong
When they put him in a cop car.
His paws couldn't reach the
pedals
So he didn't get very far.

Then, when Quincy tried to get
tough,
Criminals thought he was jokin'.
They'd say, *"Aah! How cute!
Look at his ickle suit!"*
And just want to cuddle and
stroke him.

Quincy's career ended in shame.
Fellow officers said he'd go nuts
If he didn't have coffee and a regular supply
Of eucalyptus leaf doughnuts.

It looks like the police have a really tough job.
It looks like policemen look younger.
But at least policemen don't look like
Marsupials from Down-Under.

Rusty the Squirrel

Rusty the grey squirrel
Has been lazy all his life.
He'd never go collecting nuts
To feed his kids and wife.

"Instead of trekking round the woods
I'll nip to the shop," he boasted,
"And buy a family-sized bag of
Ready Salted or Dry Roasted!"

Doo Doo the Dodo

Doo Doo the Dodo
Is the last of her kind.
Why is that? I don't know
But she was quite a find.
The population of dodos
Is currently…one.
The rest are extinct, killed off,
Quenched, all gone.
It seems that Doo Doo
Is the bird time forgot.
Why isn't she as dead
As a you know what?
The dodo called Doo Doo
Lives in my shed.

She's so sad, but you'd be
If your friends were dead.
I could've said" Shoo, shoo!"
To that poor dodo
But it seems too cruel to do,
So she won't go, go.
Doo Doo gets desperate
For dodo company.
But there are no more left
So she's had it you see.
I've tried to find another
But I just can't no way!
There's none at the zoo
And none on e-bay.
So conversation's a no-no
Which makes her "Boo Hoo!"
She's one lonely dodo,
Poor old Doo Doo.
I bought her a mirror
To help her recover.
Now my dodo is so-so
She thinks there's another!
Doo Doo now talks to
Her reflection all week
And it lifts me to see
A smile on her beak.
Now Doo Doo the Dodo
Is cheerful – not mopey.
But I can see why they died out,
They're so dodo dopey!

Super Spaniel

Is it a bird? Is it a plane?
No, it's not by heck!
It's next door's Cocker Spaniel
With a cape tied round his neck!

They call him Super Spaniel;
He isn't like the others.
As a pup he would beat up
His sisters and his brothers.

This mighty mutt has powers,
Leaps buildings in one bound!
Has x-ray eyes and radar ears
That pick up every sound!

But I wouldn't ever stroke him.
Listen, please, I beg.
You don't wanna be in the firing line
When he cocks his super leg!
He got his puppy powers
From something that he ate –
A can of "Doggy Chunks" that was
Severely out of date.

But I'm afraid to report
(And this will drive you crazy!)
He doesn't use the powers he has;
This dog is doggone lazy.

Does he use his supersonic speed
To catch thieves and put them in jail?
Nope! Just to run in circles
And try to catch his tail.

Super Spaniel has jaws of steel
But they don't get used at all.
The only action they ever see
Is chewing a squeaky ball.

And does he use his super sense of smell
To foil terrible crimes?
Nah! It's only used to sniff
Other dog's behinds.

So let this dog's tale be a lesson to you,
And, if you have powers of your own,
Don't spend your time chasing cats
Or chewing on a bone.

Be anything but ordinary,
Not just another Joe Bloggs.
Be the best that you can be
And you won't go to the dogs.

Graham the Croc

Let me tell you about Graham the Croc,
With his huge teeth, real sharp and white.
No jungle beast would go near him
In case Graham gave them a bite.

But one day Graham met a crocodile hunter
Who jumped on him with lightning pace,
And the crocodile hunter pulled Graham's teeth out,
Which wiped the smile off his face.

So Graham was left sad and toothless
And was so overcome with grief,
That he visited the jungle dentist,
To get a huuuge pair of false teeth.

So if you're visiting Graham, don't go in the day,
See him at night time instead,
As his huge teeth aren't so scary when they're
In a glass of water next to his bed!

Ooga Booga!

If you go down to the jungle
(But be careful, it's quite scary)
You might just see a monkey
Who is big and fat and hairy.

How do I know about him?
I've seen him there that's how.
The natives have a name for him,
Chant it with me now:

OOGA BOOGA! OOGA BOOGA!
OOGA BOOGA! OOGA BOOGA!

He never moves a muscle,
Just sits there all day long.
Sometimes he'll have a long nap
And dream that he's King Kong.

The natives have to feed him,
He's quite a hungry guy,
And if they don't keep food coming
He'll shout his monkey cry:

OOGA BOOGA! OOGA BOOGA!
OOGA BOOGA! OOGA BOOGA!

The natives bring heaps of fresh fruit
To feed the hairy lump.
He'll shovel it in and then let out
A banana flavoured trump.

They get fed up of feeding him
But won't monkey around,
'Cos if they stop they'll get no peace,
Just Ooga Booga's sound:

OOGA BOOGA! OOGA BOOGA!
OOGA BOOGA! OOGA BOOGA!

All night long through the treetops
And all around the jungle,
You can hear his loud voice cry
And his big tummy rumble.

"We daren't stop," one small native said,
"We're scared that he might harm us.
But this endless monkey chanting
Is driving us bananas!"

OOGA BOOGA! OOGA BOOGA!
OOGA BOOGA! OOGA BOOGA!

One day they couldn't take no more –
The natives had a plan:
"To shut this big fat monkey up
We must do what we can."

So while the ape was sleeping,
What they did was this:
They took the biggest banana they had
And shoved it up his...

OOGA BOOGA! OOGA BOOGA!
OOGA BOOGA! OOGA BOOGA!

The Little Blue Lion

Many, many miles away,
Where the land is hard and dry
And there's no escape from the sun
Burning in the sky,

There is a pride of lions
Living there together,
They eat and sleep and live their lives
Enjoying the good weather.

Most of the lions are happy,
Except one little guy;
The other lions don't like him much –
Let me tell you why.

They laugh and point and snigger,
They shout names at him too.
The reason he gets picked on is
His fur is coloured blue.

Whilst all other lions are golden,
With a brownish mane,
For some reason, we don't know why,
This lion is not the same.

When he takes a stroll through the jungle
The hyenas stop and laugh,
And it's a great big pain in the neck
To be ridiculed by a giraffe.

It makes the little lion cry,
He doesn't think it's fair
That he should be picked upon
Because he's got different hair.

Then, one day, a bright red parrot
Squawked down from her nest:
"I think that you should be quite pleased
You don't look like the rest!"

"Yes! You're right!
It's not my fault
That I am blue, not brown!
From now on I'll ignore the taunts,
I won't take this lion down!"

From this day on I'll stand up tall
And roar my message loud!
I like the fact that I am blue –
I stand out in a crowd!"

"Besides, it's not my colour,
But the lion I am inside.
When I walk through the jungle,
I'll wear my fur with pride!"

And now the other animals
Don't laugh when he walks by
Because the little blue lion
Holds his little blue head high.

Whereas before they'd shout and point,
And call him a blue freak,
Now he's the main attraction,
He's one of a kind – he's unique!

Fishin' For An Answer

Now, something that's been bugging me,
And I'd like to share with you,
Is a question I've got about fishermen
And something that they do.

Please tell me, when they catch a fish
(And sometimes it takes all day)
Why do they throw it back again
So it can swim away?

Now – don't get me wrong, it's a good thing.
As the fish gets to live and be free.
I just can't work out what the point of it is
Can somebody please help me?

Does the fisherman just want to delay him?
Does he want to make the fish late?
What if the fish had a hair appointment?
Or perhaps a red-hot date?

Just think – he might have a train to catch
Or a test booked for his eyes!
Fisherman, please leave the fish alone
So they can get on with their busy lives!

Stinkypoo the Tummy Troll

Have you ever noticed,
When you wake up from your sleep,
Your hair is in a real mess
And your clothes are in a heap?

And even though you went to bed,
Your body clean enough,
When you check your belly button
It's always full of fluff?!

You may have showered the night before
You're clean without a doubt.
But stick your finger in it
And a piece of fluff pops out?!

I'll tell you why it happens,
But keep it between me and you,
It's the work of a tummy troll
By the name of Stinkypoo!

I don't want to alarm you,
But when you fall asleep
He'll tiptoe into your bedroom,
Onto your tummy creep...

And gently, oh so gently,
With perfect grace and poise,
He'll place fluff into your naval
Without making a noise.

"Why does he do it?" I hear you ask.
Well – it's what tummy trolls do!
But that's not all you can expect
From little Stinkypoo.

Just as we are sleeping,
Stinkypoo awakes
And slowly does his nightly rounds –
And what mischief he makes!

You go to bed still wearing socks,
(A rather fetching pair,)
And wake up the next morning
To find one of your feet is bare!

Stinkypoo has made his move
And whipped it from your toes.
Where has he put it? Is it lost?
Well, no one really knows.

And even though you're sleeping sound
On sheets crisp, white and clean,
Upon opening both your eyes,
Guess which troll has been?!

He packs his little bag up
And in the night he comes,
Emptying it onto your sheets...
Grit and biscuit crumbs!

As you slowly drift to sleep
With Teddy under your arm,
His furry face, his little legs,
Keeping you safe from harm,

But WHAT!? As you awaken –
The shock! The pain! The sin!
Little Teddy's upside down
In your waste paper bin!

Then sometimes, though you go to bed
Your stomach feeling fine,
You'll wake up in the early hours
And your tummy will gurgle and whine!

Oh, the pain! The aches! The noise!
And, pwoar! What's that funny smell?
It seems that Stinkypoo has cast
His flappy-woofwoof spell!

And then his crowning glory,
So when he's gone, he's not
forgotten.
A juicy piece of fluffy stuff
Thrust in your belly button.

But don't be scared of Stinkypoo,
Don't think him bad or shocking.
He just leaves fluff in your naval at night
Like Santa leaves gifts in your stocking.

So the next time you wake one fine morning
With crumbs and grit in your bed,
One sock gone missing, your bear in your bin
Or a smell like your gerbil is dead,

Check your belly button,
And if the fluff is packed in tight,
I'd say Stinkypoo the Tummy Troll
Paid you a visit last night!

Phillipe the Furry French Fox

Phillipe the Furry French Fox
Fancied something to eat
So he strolled to his favourite French restaurant
Where he sat in his favourite seat.

The waiter appeared with his notepad.
"Would you care for some hotdogs today?"
But Phillipe the Furry French Fox replied,
"I want snails – bring them right away!"

The waiter returned with the snails,
Phillipe slurped them all down.
Said the waiter, "Would you care for some burgers now?"
But Phillipe replied with a frown:

"No, no, no! Bring me more snails!"
The waiter did as he was told.
Phillipe the Furry French Fox
Ate them all up, slimy and cold.

"For the final course, Monsieur," the waiter enquired,
"How about the finest pizza ever made?"
Phillipe shook his head, "More snails!" he said.
They came, then he ate, then he paid.

As the fox left the restaurant, the
waiter grabbed him
Saying, "Sir, I don't mean
to be rude,
But how come snails are all that
you eat?"
Phillipe said, "I don't like
fast food."

Never Feed Ducks Jelly Babies

Never feed ducks jelly babies,
It makes them mad and see red.
It's because they have no teeth in their beaks
To bite off their little heads.

And never feed ducks garlic bread,
It always makes them wish
They'd not had it the night before,
As they can't creep up on fish.

And never feed ducks burgers,
Not even for a treat.
It's not easy picking gherkins out
When you've only got webbed feet.

And never, ever, EVER
Give ducks fine cheese and wine
They develop quite a taste for it
And then have it all the time.

QUACK!!

HIC!!

Rory the Dinosaur

Rory the Dinosaur was a huge scaly beast,
The scariest monster you'd meet.
Sharp claws, large teeth and 60ft tall,
If you measure him in his stocking feet.

The cavemen all call him Rory,
Because of his deafening ROOOOAARRRR!!!
And if Rory was in the mood to fight,
He'd make any dino-sore.

His hobbies were terrorizing others,
His reputation is known countrywide.
He's scared Stegosaurus, beat up Brontosaurus,
And left Pterodactyls pterrified!

Then one day a tiny mosquito
Landed on Rory's large snout
Saying, "Just 'cos you're large you don't have to be hard,
Why don't you just try chilling out?!"

"You speak big words little insect!" Rory said.
"But you're right – I should control my rage
I'll try to be calm and not cause any harm,
My aggressions left in the Stone Age!"

So now Rory's more pleasant to be around.
He has friends and his hobbies are changing.
No more biting or hitting, instead he does knitting
And takes classes in flower arranging!

UG!

Pull up stone and listen.
My name is UG! – ok?
They call me UG! coz only word
My Mum and Dad could say.

UG! thought he write a poem.
It take a while I bet.
I'm writing with a chisel –
There are no pencils yet.

My only clothes are leopard fur;
Nothing ever fits.
I wish someone make Y-fronts
To warm my chilly bits.

This morning UG! invent wheel,
Afternoon invented car
But tomorrow inventing traffic jam
So not get very far.

It boring being caveman,
Not much to do at all.
Until someone invent T.V.
Me just draw on the wall.

Me rent a little cave for one,
One day I like to buy.
But must meet Mrs UG! first
As mortgages sky high!

But women say UG! hairy
And they not like it when I belch!
But they all ugly anyway
Except that Raquel Welch.

UG! had pet pterodactyl
With huge wings and big beak.
Me had to have him put down though –
He ate Grandma last week.

Me really got to go now,
UG! have to get hair right.
UG!'s friends are coming round soon –
We going clubbing tonight!

Simon and Sue

Simon was a worker ant
Who had a lovely wife.
The pair of ants were proud parents
And had a busy life.

So when the chance came for a night on the town
Simon and Sue couldn't wait.
They hurriedly arranged a babysitter
For their kids, all one hundred and eight.

The sitter arrived; they sped out the door,
Not giving him a glance,
And so he was left in a room for the night
Looking after all the little ants.

The hours ticked by, Sue and Simon came home,
Just imagine their shock and their pain
As they realised they'd left their kids in the care
Of a hairy ant-eater called Wayne!

Stinkerbell the Toothy Peg Fairy

Stinkypoo here, to tell you a rhyme
About a really good friend of mine
Called Stinkerbell who, if you didn't know,
Takes the spare teeth from beneath your pillow.
She'll fly in the window in the middle of the night
And float onto your duvet while snuggled up tight.
She'll take all your old toothy pegs while asleep
And leave you some money that's all yours to keep.
And when she gets home with the teeth that she's got
She'll throw them all into a great melting pot
Which she stirs, boils and moulds with all of her might
To build a huge castle all shiny and white.
That gets larger daily, rooms too many to mention;
She'll be coming your way soon – she wants an extension!
She'll sit in her castle quite a happy fellow,
Brushing it twice a day so it doesn't go yellow.

(Just one word of warning when you're in bed at night
Don't put your pillow on your head.
As she'll steal all your gnashers and leave you lying there
With a mouthful of gums instead!)

161

The Day it Sounded Different

I knew that day when I woke up
Something wasn't right.
I think it was when my dog meowed
As I switched on the light.

"What's happening?" I thought as I ran downstairs
(After brushing my teeth of course!)
I sat down for breakfast, said "Morning!" to Mum
And she neighed at me like a big horse.

The bees in the garden were honking like geese!
The birds in the trees made me jump!
They were mooing like cows as I poured out my milk
And my cereal went Snap! Crackle! Trump!

I quickly got dressed and headed for school
But as I scurried down the street
All the people jabbered like monkeys
And the car horns were going Tweet! Tweet!

I met my best friend in the classroom and said,
"Something's happening of great note!"
He stared at me, opened his mouth,
Then bleated like a goat!

We sat in our seats – the teacher came in,
A cat outside started squeaking!
The class hamster lay clucking in his cage
As my teacher started speaking...

Then, even after all the strange sounds I'd heard,
This one made me more worried and tense.
I couldn't believe it! Imagine my surprise
As my teacher talked some sense!!

The Bear in my Wardrobe

There's a bear that lives in my wardrobe,
He keeps trying on my clothes.
He pulls on my shirt and jumper,
Wipes my hanky on his nose.
My trousers he'll yank over his stubby legs,
Tries socks on pair after pair.
Sometimes he'll fling the doors open wide
And run round in my underwear.
The bear I have no objection to,
Even though I think he's insane.
It's just that after he's tried my clothes on
Nothing fits me again!

Brad Beaver

The beavers swam and worked and played
In the river deep.
They built their little beaver dams
In which they all could sleep.

The dams were all damn sturdy,
Could withstand storm or flood,
Except dams built by Brad Beaver –
At construction he wasn't too good.

In some dams beaver discos were held,
Where boy and girl beavers connected.
But Brad's dams were that bad, to keep them held up,
Scaffolding would be erected.

In other dams, maths lessons were taught,
Teachers and pupils would mix.
But the conclusion was always… *Strong wind + Brad's dams
= big pile of sticks.*

Whilst other fine homes held book clubs,
(Reading *Stumpy's Big Adventure* perhaps?)
Brad's attempts to look at his favourite book
Would end up with his home in collapse.

But those days are gone! Brad now lives in a home
Without any worry or fear!
With a few nails and glue, his home's now brand new!
A flat-pack dam fresh from IKEA!

Harold

Harold was a slippery snake
Who always shed his skin.
Every month he got a new
Body to live in.

He had so many empty suits,
Do you know what he did?
He took them to a car boot sale
And made almost ten quid!

Stinkypoo and Fang Too

Stinkypoo sat in his house one day,
Moulding his fluff into mounds.
His bag of grit and biscuit crumbs
Was packed for his nightly rounds.

When all of a sudden – a bang on the door!
The tummy toll wondered. "Who's that?"
He opened it up and there on his step
Was a bug-eyed, big-toothed battered bat.

His name was Fang the Fruit Bat.
He'd come to have a look
For a companion and someone to care
(He'd been searching throughout this whole book!)

Stinkypoo took him in at once
And laid him in some fluff,
"I'll go and get you some food," he said,
"You're looking pretty rough."

Stinkypoo offered fluff sandwiches
And a slice of peepy meat.
But the bat just turned his nose up
And refused to try and eat.

In fact Fang had already decided
He didn't think this place was swell...
It was full of fluff, odd socks and crumbs
And it had a trumpy smell.

So off he flew through the window
To continue searching about.
Will he find a friend before the end of the book?
Well – you'll have to keep reading to find out!

I'm Bathing my Dog

I'm bathing my dog,
He's standing in a tub.
He's having a good clean
And getting a rub.

He's so wet and bedraggled
He looks like he's drowned!
But he really enjoys it…
Hang on…what's that sound?

My dog's ears pricked up.
He heard it too.
I'll just carry on
With his doggy shampoo…

The soap in my hands
Is all slippy and slidey…
OH NO! NOT AGAIN!!

PIDEY! PIDEY!! PIDEY!!!!!

The Hole in the Sky

Whilst walking along the other day
I noticed a hole in the sky.
I'm sure it wasn't there the day before,
So I began to wonder why...

I stared at the hole whilst trying to avoid
A woman collecting for the poor
But in doing so I nearly tripped over
A homeless man in a shop door.

I walked past some teenagers fighting
And a child driving his parents spare,
All of this time still pondering,
"Why is that big hole up there?"

Past walls of graffiti I wandered still,
Through a derelict housing estate.
I strolled as far as a burnt-out car
Where an old tramp sat on a crate.

I turned to the haggard old man and asked,
"What is that big hole I see?"
He said with a sigh, "Son, that hole in the sky,
Is the place where God used to be..."

Never Put Parents Up Your Nose

Never put parents up your nose,
Clever it is not.
You'll just end up with a sticky Mum
And a Dad covered in snot.

John Wallaby

John Wallaby loved to play golf,
He thought the game was neat,
But he got quite chilly on the course,
Especially round his feet.

So his wife (the lovely Wilma)
Knitted some socks for John.
But when he got on the golf course
He got a hole in one.

Slug and Centipede

There was once this slug and this centipede
And it really was no joke
The money problems that they had –
These insects were flat broke.

They hatched a plan together
To try to make things right;
The plan was to rob the local bank,
Late on Tuesday night.

The slug and the centipede talked it through
So there wasn't any mistake.
They planned it all so carefully,
From the break-in to their escape.

That Tuesday night, while other bugs
Were tucked up in their beds,
Slug and Centipede were in the bank
With tights upon their heads.

The slug couldn't carry much money
But the plan still worked like a charm
As the centipede shoved a big bag of cash
Under every arm.

They got away with thousands
And they thought that that was that,
But, I'm afraid, the police planned a raid
On their East End flat.

The police, you see, found two vital clues,
So the insects' chances were slim;
The centipede left many finger prints
And the slug left a trail behind him.

Ode to a Dead Cat

My cat is dead! My cat is dead!
Poor kitty is no more.
He's starting to whiff, he's cold and he's stiff,
Lying on my kitchen floor.

My cat is gone! My cat is gone!
Old kitty is starting to harden.
He's flat out in his tray, but soon he will lay
In a hole at the end of the garden.

Jigsaw

My grandma loves to do jigsaws,
She'll do them all the day.
Until she's finished the one she's on,
Nothing gets in her way.

She'll spread it on her table,
Sit with a cup of tea
And not move 'til it's completed
(Or until her soaps come on TV).

The jigsaws are of anything:
A barn owl, a red setter,
A book, a hen, a duck, a pen,
The more pieces the better.

There's one particular jigsaw,
It's a picture of a deer,
She just can't seem to finish it,
She's been doing it all year.

It was January when she started,
Slowly, bit by bit,
And now it's late September
And she still can't finish it.

Every day and every night
The jigsaw will not end.
I think it's driving grandma mad!
She's going round the bend!

I can sometimes hear her in the night,
Cackling with the strain.
She'll throw the jigsaw on the floor,
Pick it up and start again...

I know why she'll never finish it.
But she won't hear it from me:
Two pieces were sucked up the hoover
And the dog's eaten at least three!!

Never Put Pets Up Your Nose

Never put pets up your nose,
It's dangerous and naughty.
Though you think you will not see them again
They'll fall back down when you're forty.

Shark in the Toilet!

SHARK IN THE TOILET! SHARK IN THE TOILET!
Please listen to what's on my mind!
It's not good for your health when you relieve yourself
And a shark bites you on the behind!

I don't know how long he's been in there
I just know that I let out a shriek!
When I sat down to go to the toilet
And he nibbled me on my left cheek!

SHARK IN THE TOILET! SHARK IN THE TOILET!
It's shocked me to my very soul!
I couldn't believe how his big jaws smiled back
As I peered into the bowl.

Now I don't want to startle you too much,
But things are looking quite grim.
He just sort of chuckled at me
As I threw rolls of Andrex at him!

SHARK IN THE TOILET! SHARK IN THE TOILET!
I'm beginning to think I can't win!
I just bopped him with a bog brush
But he sliced it in half with his fin!

I can't think how to get rid of him;
I've run out of toilet rolls and brushes.
He just sort of bobs back to the surface
Even after two or three flushes!

SHARK IN THE TOILET! SHARK IN THE TOILET!
Won't someone please listen to me!
We have to get rid of him right now:
I *really* have to pee!!

Elvis the Ugly Baby

"MY GOD YOU ARE UGLY!" were the first words he heard.
As the hospital ward went wild.
And it has to be said that the doctor was right –
It was one *ugly* child.

He lay in his cot, dribbling and
gurgling,
The nurses brought blankets of cotton.
He was so ugly it took half an hour
To work out which end was his bottom.

His parents still loved him; they thought he was cute,
Well, that's what the both of them said.
They called their son Elvis as he had no hair,
Except for a quiff on his head.

They took him for walks in their local
park,
He threw bread for the ducks,
But the ducks just threw the bread
straight back
When they saw his hideous looks.

Other parents would peer in his pram
Then run away real quick,
And if they'd recently had a meal
Odds on, they'd be sick.

The old Playschool was the grandest building
You had ever seen.
Huge windows, polished floors,
The odd old wooden beam.

Its crumbling walls had seen some kids,
Some pleasant – some making a fuss.
But was this old Playschool ready for one
That looked like the back end of a bus?

On his first morning there, Elvis couldn't wait
To draw and build and paint,
But the other kids would cry and scream,
And most of the teachers would faint.

His parents would not give up though,
They sent him back once more.
"Our son deserves to build with blocks,
And read and play and draw!"

Again the classroom erupted!
His classmates yelled and cried!
And when Elvis met the class hamster,
The hamster keeled over and died!

The teachers called a meeting,
And to the parents they said,
"The only way we can have your son back
Is if he comes with a bag on his head."

Elvis' parents trudged out the school
To break the news to their son.
And there was Elvis smiling and jumping,
Having so much fun!

"What's happened darling?" Mother asked,
"I've never seen you so happy!"
Elvis just smiled a contented smile
Then did a brown mess in his nappy.

The reason Elvis was satisfied
Was that he'd found a friend,
Someone who'd stick right by his side
Until the bitter end.

"WHAT IS IT?!?" screamed his father,
"It looks like a giant blister!"
"No," said the nurse that was holding it,
"It's Elvis' ugly sister!"

"It turns out you have had twins,
We thought that perhaps, maybe,
She was yours – but it took this long,
To work out it's a baby!"

So there they were – the ugly twins,
A sister and a brother,
Both now happy to be ugly,
As they both look as bad as each other.

They play together, blissfully happy,
Running round the park.
(They just don't mix with other kids,
And they go out when it's dark.)

And the old Playschool is quiet once more,
From its floor to its intricate gilding,
Because Elvis has left the reading and painting
And Elvis has left the building...

Barnaby Wilde the Rock 'n' Roll Worm

Barnaby Wilde is a Rock 'n' Roll Worm,
To be famous is his goal.
He was born to entertain a crowd
With soil, bugs and rock 'n' roll!

Barnaby's always dreamed of the top,
Right from the day of his birth.
He thinks his talent is far too big
To be buried in the earth.

But, alas, his career will never take off.
This worm won't become a star.
Despite all his charms – he hasn't got arms,
To play his electric guitar.

BITEY:REVAMPED

A full moon lit up the black sky as the clock ticked round
to midnight.
A flapping noise filled the graveyard – a vampire was
in flight!
In front of the moon, a silhouette appeared
(that looked just a tad overweight!)
And a revamped Bitey the Veggie Vampire flitted over
the cemetery gate.

The gravedigger said," I knew he'd rise again –
I could feel it in my bones.
That Veggie Vampire makes more comebacks
than the Rolling Stones!"
"Good luck Bitey!" he shouted, and waved Bitey off
as he flew,
"I hope" he yelled," That this resurrection goes better
than the last two!"

Bitey shot straight home, really fast, like a bullet
from a gun,
He'd not eaten food for a couple of years, and boy –
he wanted some!
He flew in the door feeling tired and hungry –
his stomach making a din,
And began searching his cupboards for grub
(something without garlic in.)

But before Bitey could find some food, a thought
flashed through his head,
"Perhaps I should quit being veggie? Should I start
eating meat instead?
Could the reason I die so much be because I don't eat
like the rest?
I'm the only Veggie Vampire I know – perhaps drinking
blood is best?"

"Do I stick to my principals and stay veggie?
Would that be such a disaster?
Do I sling the salad and bite some necks?
Should I nibble people or pasta?"
Then all of a sudden – a THUD! at the door…
"Who's there?" Bitey cried,
Lying there was a battered bat, who looked like
he might have just died.

Bitey took the bat inside, gently stroking his head.
He knew all too well what it felt like, to feel half alive
and half dead.
After a while the bat opened his eyes and slowly unfolded
his wings.
Bitey rushed to bring insects and other meaty things.

But the bat refused to eat any meat – he preferred
some parsnip stew!
Bitey rejoiced and danced around - the bat was a veggie too!
They both became bat buddies – it really was meant to be!
Bitey and Fang – forever friends, both alone
in the world…and veggie!

They ate a huge feast to celebrate and once they had
that full feeling
They fell asleep – side by side – hanging from the ceiling.
When they awoke, Bitey said, "To the park! A picnic with
veggie treats!"
They prepared some quiche, a salad, some fruit and
sandwiches full of fake meats.

Carrying the hamper they flew out the door,
feeling revamped and reborn,
And having such a laugh that they didn't notice the day
had started to dawn…

They got to the park, but it wasn't too long before
Bitey got into a fix,
With all the excitement of Fang, he forgot that vampires
and sunshine don't mix...

He tossed a stick through the air for Fang –
the bat brought it back in a flash,
But where Bitey had been, all that could be seen,
was a pile of smouldering ash...

Now Bitey rests in pieces... let's have silence for a minute...
And raise some quiche to his memory
(just be sure there's no meat in it)
He may have been tubby – he did die a lot –
but he tried the best that he could.
He was Bitey the Veggie Vampire –
who wasn't very good...